TIMELINES OF
AMERICAN HISTORY ™

A Timeline of the White House

Lisa Modifica

The Rosen Publishing Group, Inc., New York

Published in 2004 by The Rosen Publishing Group, Inc.
29 East 21st Street, New York, NY 10010

First Edition

Library of Congress Cataloging-in-Publication Data

Modifica, Lisa.
A timeline of the White House/Lisa Modifica—1st ed.
        p. cm.—(Timelines of American history)
Summary: Provides a chronological look at major events in the history of the White House, from the planning for its construction at the end of the eighteenth century up to the 1990s.
Includes bibliographical references and index.
ISBN 0-8239-4543-X (library binding)
1. White House (Washington, D.C.)—History—Chronology—Juvenile literature.
2. Presidents—United States—History—Chronology—Juvenile literature. 3. Washington (D.C.)—Buildings, structures, etc.—Juvenile literature. [1. White House (Washington, D.C.)—History—Chronology. 2. Presidents—History—Chronology.] I. Title. II. Series.
F204.W5M63 2004
975.3—dc22

                                                                    2003015648

Manufactured in the United States of America

On the cover: An image of the White House
On the title page: Plan from 1791 of Washington, D.C., by Pierre-Charles L'Enfant

Contents

1

The Early Years of the White House

When it was built, the "President's House" was the largest mansion in America. George Washington chose Pierre-Charles L'Enfant, the city planner of Washington, D.C., to design the house. L'Enfant was fired because his design was too fancy and he argued too much. Then Washington selected James Hoban for the

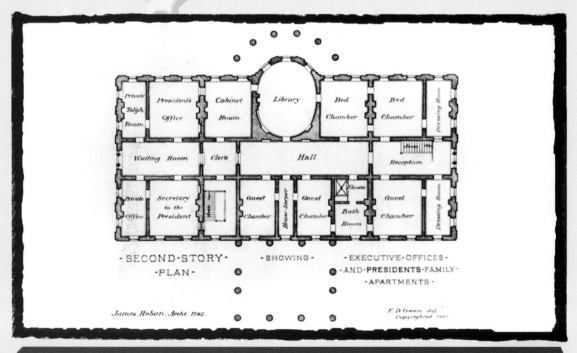

The floor plan of the second floor of the White House. The plans were drawn up by Irish architect James Hoban in 1792. Hoban, who was born in Ireland in 1762, came to the United States in 1789.

job. His design was much smaller than L'Enfant's and looked like a house although it was still the largest mansion in America.

BUILDING THE FIRST WHITE HOUSE

WASHINGTON D.C. 1798
MODERN
WASHINGTON
is served by the
PENNSYLVANIA RAILROAD

Above is an image of the White House under construction from September 28, 1931.

★ **1790**

The Residence Act of 1790 is passed. This act makes George Washington responsible for setting up the new capital of the United States. It also sets the first Monday of December 1800 as the deadline for finishing the President's House.

★ **1792**

George Washington selects the site of the new capital. The spot has a beautiful view of the Potomac River. Thomas Jefferson places advertisements in local newspapers asking for designs of the president's new house. The winner receives $500 or a gold medal. George Washington selects architect James Hoban's design for the presidential house and construction begins.

★ **1798**

The walls of the President's House are whitewashed for the first time.

★ **1800**

The U.S. capital is officially moved from Philadelphia to Washington, D.C.

Moving In

When John Adams moved into the President's House, it was still under construction. The house had thirty-six rooms, but most of them were unusable. Adams's wife, Abigail, used one of the rooms to dry her laundry. Workers built bridges in the yard so that the president could walk around without getting his feet dirty. The roof leaked, and

This 1807 drawing by Henry Latrobe shows the east side of the White House. The north and south porticoes seen here were built later, but with some minor changes. A portico is a porch or walkway with a roof that is supported by columns. Porticoes often lead to the entrance of a building.

for a bathroom, the residents used an outhouse. The Adamses lived in the President's House for only four months, and they were never very comfortable there. When Thomas Jefferson moved in, he worked hard to make it inviting and comfortable.

1800
John Adams, the second president of the United States, and his wife, Abigail, are the first people to move into the President's House.

1801
Thomas Jefferson moves into the President's House. Jefferson continues

President John Adams

the tradition of public tours of the President's House. He also holds public receptions on New Year's Day and the Fourth of July.

1809
Although not very old, the President's House is in need of work and repairs begin. Architect Benjamin H. Latrobe is put in charge.

1811
A British diplomat calls the President's House the "White House" in writing for the first time.

7

Fire at the White House

Dolley Madison (the wife of President J. Madison) was a smart woman. Though the War of 1812 was on and the British were coming to attack, Dolley would not leave the White House until she packed the original Declaration of Independence and the Constitution. The frame around artist Gilbert Stuart's portrait of George Washington was too heavy to lift off the wall, so Dolley Madison had the portrait cut out and packed as well.

★ **1812**
James Madison declares war on Great Britain. Great Britain has been capturing American ships and blocking American harbors.

★ **1814**
The British burn several buildings in Washington, D.C., including the Capitol and the White House. Before they set the White House on fire, the soldiers eat the meal that had been made for the president. They also steal several things from the White House. Luckily, a heavy rainstorm puts out the fire. But the only part to survive is the outer stone wall and the basement. A relative of one of the British soldiers will return some of the stolen items years later.

★ **1815**
James Hoban, the original architect, is hired to

8

This image shows Dolley Madison—wife of fourth president James Madison—in her heroic attempt to save important government papers and a portrait of George Washington during the British invasion of Washington, D.C.

rebuild the White House. The reconstruction costs as much as it originally cost to build the house.

1817 ★
President James Monroe moves into the unfinished White House.

2

Life at the White House

The White House has been through many renovations. Though it had only a few rooms that could be lived in during President Adams's time, now it has 6 floors, 132 rooms, 35 bathrooms, 147 windows, 412 doors, 12 chimneys, 8 staircases, and 3 elevators.

The White House has also lived through many other kinds of changes. New inventions became a part of the house. For example, though it is hard to imagine, not all of the presidents and their families had running water or heat.

This is a view of the ballroom at the White House during the second inauguration of Abraham Lincoln.

★ **1825**

President John Quincy Adams plants the first flower garden at the White House.

★ **1829**

Andrew Jackson is inaugurated as the seventh president of the United States. Jackson is the first president who is not from a wealthy family. At his inauguration party, Jackson's guests break and dirty White House furniture. Jackson escapes out a window when the party gets out of control.

★ **1833**

Running water is installed at the White House.

★ **1850**

Abigail Fillmore, the wife of President Millard Fillmore, begins the White House Library. She chooses books for the library, which is located in an upstairs room. Also in the room are her harp, guitar, and piano.

President Andrew Jackson is shown taking the oath of office on March 4, 1829.

★ **1865**

President Abraham Lincoln is the first U.S. president to be assassinated.

11

Sharing the White House

There have always been many parties at the White House. It is the president's job to entertain foreign visitors and politicians. The president also honors people who have made great achievements in their lives. He gives out many awards to people and invites celebrities to perform at the White House. The first family understands that it and the White House are important symbols to Americans. The first family often holds special events that the general public can enjoy. An example is the yearly White House Easter Egg Roll.

★ **July 5, 1865**
The U.S. Secret Service, part of the United States Department of Treasury, is established. Its first job is to go after criminals who make fake money.

★ **1867**
The role of the Secret Service expands to include looking out for criminals who steal mail, smuggle, and commit other crimes against federal laws.

★ **1878**
First Lady Lucy Hayes (wife of President Rutherford B. Hayes) holds an Easter egg–rolling competition on the front lawn of the White House. The activity becomes an annual event and is still celebrated today.

A photo of the Easter Egg Roll at the White House on April 5, 1926. The original site of the Easter Egg Roll was at the grounds of the United States Capitol. Other egg-related games—Egg Picking, Egg Ball, Toss and Catch, and Egg Croquet—were popular on Easter Monday.

Shown here is the marriage of Grover Cleveland and Frances Folsom.

1878 ★

Many trees are planted while Rutherford B. Hayes is president. Planting trees every time a new president is elected becomes a tradition.

1886 ★

President Grover Cleveland marries Frances Folsom. He is the first and only president who is married in the White House. Cleveland was elected as president again in 1893. He served until 1897.

13

Being the President

Living in the White House is very nice, but being a president is hard work. After the assassination of President William McKinley, the role of the Secret Service expanded to include full-time protection of the president. Though this helped to keep the president safe, it was hard for the president and his family since people were always following them. From then on, presidents would have little privacy.

1901
Electric lights are added to the White House. President William McKinley is assassinated in Buffalo, New York. He is the third president to be assassinated.

1902
President Theodore Roosevelt works with architect Charles McKim to renovate the entire White House. The Executive Office Building is built. The Executive Office Building contains offices for the president and his staff. It is later called the West Wing. Theodore Roosevelt orders "White House" to be printed on his stationery. The White House becomes the official name of the mansion.

This is the Red Room at the White House during President William McKinley's administration.

1906

Protecting the president officially becomes the job of the Secret Service.

1908

President Roosevelt transfers eight Secret Service agents to the Department of Justice. These agents become the start of the Federal Bureau of Investigation (FBI).

1909

William Howard Taft, the twenty-seventh president, purchases the first official automobiles of the White House. In order to house them, the stable is knocked down and a garage is built in its place.

President William Howard Taft and his wife, First Lady Helen Herron Taft, take a ride in the backseat of a convertible. These cars were the first White House automobiles. President Taft was born on September 15, 1857, in Cincinnati, Ohio.

3

The White House and the Outside World

The early twentieth century brought more changes to the White House. New inventions were added inside the house and another branch of the Secret Service was formed. This branch guarded the vice president, his family, and any visiting foreign diplomats. George Washington's plan of making the White House open to the public still existed, but with so many visitors, guarding the White House, the president, the vice president, and their families was difficult.

1922

The White House gets electric vacuum cleaners. President Warren G. Harding adds a radio to the book-case in his study.

Harding forms the Uniformed Division of the Secret Service. The Uniformed Division—originally called the White House Police—protects the White House, the president, the vice president, and their families.

President Warren G. Harding

Shown here is the messy scene at the Executive Mansion, which underwent repairs in January 1930. Scaffolding on the façade of the building covers damage that was caused by a fire.

1926 ★

The White House gets an electric refrigerator. Before that, iceboxes had been used in the White House.

1929 ★

A fire destroys the inside of the West Wing.

1933 ★

The *New York Daily News* raises $40,000 to build an indoor swimming pool for President Franklin D. Roosevelt. Though Roosevelt lost the use of his legs in 1921, he was able to swim and he enjoyed doing so. Part of the money for the pool came from pennies collected by students.

The White House Goes Public

Before television was invented, people only knew what the president looked like from photographs and drawings. Once presidents started appearing on television, they began hiring people to help them sound smart and look good. After all, they had to make a good impression on the public. The president now has people that help write his speeches and other people that tell him what to wear.

★ **1933**
President Franklin D. Roosevelt begins his "fireside chats." These are weekly radio broadcasts to the public from the Diplomatic Reception Room at the White House. Because President Roosevelt cannot use his legs or travel a lot, he creates the chats so that the American people will get to know him.

First Lady Eleanor Roosevelt (*right*)

1934
Eleanor Roosevelt is the first president's wife to hold her own press conferences. She allows only women reporters to attend. The first lady also traveled all over the country, gave lectures and radio broadcasts, and wrote her opinions in a daily newspaper column called "My Day."

18

President Franklin Delano Roosevelt addresses the nation on the radio on October 12, 1939. Roosevelt, who became president during the Depression, promised that things would get better. As he said in his inauguration speech, "The only thing we have to fear is fear itself."

1939 ★

President Franklin D. Roosevelt is the first president to appear on television at the opening of the New York World's Fair.

1942 ★

A movie theater is added to the White House.

4

Inside the White House

When Theodore Roosevelt came to office in 1901, the White House needed a lot of work. Workers rebuilt the living area and updated the plumbing and electricity. But by the time Harry S. Truman's presidency began, the White House was in bad shape again. Truman wasn't allowed to sleep in his bedroom or use his bathroom. Many people thought the White House should be destroyed. However, Truman wanted to preserve the White House. Workers removed everything except the original brick walls and then rebuilt the White House room by room.

★ **1947**
President Harry S. Truman gives the first presidential address on television from the White House.

★ **1947**
The people of Missouri—President Truman's home state—pay for two bowling lanes to be built in the basement of the White House. Since then the lanes have been moved twice, but there are still bowling lanes in the White House.

On television, President Harry S. Truman talks to the nation after the death of President Franklin Roosevelt in 1945. Truman, who was born in 1884 in Lamar, Missouri, was the thirty-third president of the United States.

1948 ★

During Harry S. Truman's presidency, a major renovation begins. For most of Truman's presidency, he is not able to live in the White House.

1951 ★

The Secret Service becomes a permanent part of the federal government. The president and his family members each have a member of the Secret Service that guards them.

Work and Fun at the White House

Living in the White House can be stressful. The president has to make difficult decisions and work many hours. It is hard to escape these things because the president lives in the same place that he works in. Most people go to work, but then they come home and relax. Many presidents make additions to the White House, such as an exercise room, a tennis court, or a game room, so that they can relax and have some fun.

Even presidents need to relax! President Truman and his daughter Margaret play piano in 1942.

★ 1952

The Truman renovation is completed. The inside of the White House has been redone, and there are two new underground floors. President Truman takes the public on a televised tour of the White House. At this time, about 11 percent of U.S. families owned a television set.

★ 1954

The U.S. Golf Association installs a putting green on the White House lawn for President Dwight D. Eisenhower.

★ 1955

A presidential news conference is recorded and televised for the first time. President Dwight D. Eisenhower is the first president to be on color television when he appears on the *Home Show*.

★ 1960

John F. Kennedy and Richard Nixon hold four televised public debates.

Republican vice president Richard Nixon (*left*) and Democratic senator John F. Kennedy participate in a debate on television as part of their presidential campaign.

5. Getting into the White House

Many people saw the White House for the first time when First Lady Jacqueline Kennedy held a televised tour. Mrs. Kennedy had just finished a restoration of the White House and wanted to show it off. She found furniture that had originally been in the White House, had it fixed, and put it back. She tried to restore rooms so that they were the same as when they were first built. She thought that the White House should have many of the beautiful things it had when it was first built.

First Lady Jacqueline Kennedy during the televised tour of the White House, which was taped by CBS on January 13, 1962. The program went on the air in February of that year, and 80 million viewers watched it.

1962

Jacqueline Bouvier Kennedy, the wife of President John F. Kennedy, leads a tour of the White House for television. This tour gets many Americans interested in the White House.

1963

President John F. Kennedy is assassinated. A few days later, his killer is assassinated on live television.

1974

President Richard Nixon is the first, and only, president to resign his office.

February 17, 1974

An army mechanic named Robert K. Preston, lands his helicopter on the South Lawn.

December 25, 1974

A man who says he has explosives crashes into the White House gates. Nobody is hurt.

1975

A new outdoor pool is built during Gerald Ford's presidency. The original pool had been covered up during Richard Nixon's term in office.

Security at the White House

The White House is protected in many different ways. There are gates and walls, cameras and guards. People who are hired to keep the president and his family safe monitor everything. There are metal detectors at the doors. Dogs who are trained to smell explosives

sniff cars that come to the White House. The FBI checks all the people who work at the White House very carefully to ensure that everyone there is safe.

In March 2003, before the war with Iraq, extra guards were brought to the White House to protect against possible terrorist attacks. These men are from the U.S. Park Police.

1976

Six different people try to break in to the White House. None succeed in harming President Gerald Ford or the White House.

1985

Robert Latta easily walks into the White House on the day of Ronald Reagan's second inauguration. Latta wants to see the White House and there are no tours, so he sneaks in with a band of musicians who are performing.

1993

President Bill Clinton gets e-mail at the White House. He is the first president with an e-mail account.

1994

Frank Eugene Corder crashes a small plane into the South Lawn. There is minor damage to the house and nobody except Corder is hurt.

President Bill Clinton, the first president to be online in the White House, writes an e-mail to astronaut John Glenn who is aboard the space shuttle *Discovery*. The shuttle landed safely the next day.

1995

Pennsylvania Avenue in front of the White House is closed to all motor vehicles.

Learning About History with Timelines

Sometimes we use a timeline when we want to learn about history. A timeline is a list of important things that have happened. A timeline is helpful because it lists events in order. You can use a timeline to see what happened during a certain year or period. You can also use a timeline to learn what happened because of a certain event. By adding or subtracting, you can see how many years passed between one event and another. Reading a timeline is a quick way to learn about a person, place, or thing.

Glossary

architect (AR-kih-tekt) Someone who designs buildings or large structures.

assassinate (uh-SAS-sih-nayt) To murder someone.

construction (kun-STRUK-shun) Building or making something.

diplomat (DIH-pluh-mat) Someone in a government who is working with other governments.

harbor (HAR-bor) A place in the water where boats or ships can anchor.

inauguration (ih-naw-gyuh-RAY-shun) The swearing in of a new president.

permanent (PER-muh-nint) Something that stays the same.

preserve (prih-ZURV) To keep something like new.

putting (PUH-ting) Hitting a golf ball gently to the hole from a close range.

reaction (ree-AK-shun) A response to something that happens.

reception (re-SEP-shun) A party for a particular reason.

renovate (REH-noh-vayt) To make something like new.

resign (rih-ZYN) To give up a position.

restore (reh-STOR) To make something like it was before.

Web Sites

Due to the changing nature of Internet links, The Rosen
Publishing Group, Inc., has developed an online list of Web sites
related to the subject of this book. This site is updated regularly.
Please use this link to access the list:

http://www.rosenlinks.com/tah/whho

Index

A Timeline of the White House

Credits

About the author: Lisa Modifica is a freelance writer.

Photo credits: cover © Lee Snider/Corbis; pp. 1, 16 © Corbis; pp. 4, 5, 6, 10, 11, 13, 15, 17 © Library of Congress Prints and Photographs Division; p. 7 © pp. 9, 18, 22, 24 © Bettmann/Corbis; pp. 14, 19, 21, 23 © Hulton Archive/Getty Images; p. 26 © Reuters NewMedia Inc./ Corbis; p. 27 © AFP/Corbis.

Designer: Geri Fletcher; Editor: Annie Sommers